NATIONAL GEOGRAPHIC

# Corn

Marvin Buckley

# Do you like eating **corn**?

Corn is grown from seeds.
Corn can be used to make
different things.

How does corn
become all these things?

Farmers plant the corn seeds.
They use a machine called a row planter to plant the seeds in rows.

This corn plant will take four to six months to grow.

Farmers pick the corn with a machine called a corn combine. This machine picks the cobs from the corn plants and takes the corn kernels off the cobs.

The corn is loaded into grain wagons.
Then it is taken to factories.
The corn is used to make different things.

Some corn is ground up and used
to make food for farm animals.
Farmers give this food to their pigs, cattle, and sheep.

Some corn is ground up and used to make cornflakes.

Some corn is made
into cornstarch.
Cornstarch is mixed
with other things
to make paper.

Some corn is ground into cornmeal.
Cornmeal is used to make tortillas.

Some corn is made into corn syrup. Corn syrup is used to make candy.

Some corn is used
to make ethanol.
Ethanol can be added to gasoline
to make it work better.

Corn is used for other things, too.
Do you know what this corn is used for?

It’s used for

**popcorn**!

# Glossary

| | |
|---|---|
| cornflakes | a breakfast cereal made from corn |
| corn syrup | a thick, sweet liquid made from cornstarch |
| cornmeal | a flour-like grain made from corn |
| cornstarch | a white flour made from corn |
| ethanol | a type of alcohol made from corn and used for industrial purposes |
| gasoline | a liquid that is used as fuel in motor vehicles |
| tortillas | a thin, flat bread made from corn |